HAIRSTYLES

40 Amazing Princess Hairstyles
With Step by Step Images

EDDA USA

HAIRSTYLES

40 Amazing Princess Hairstyles
With Step by Step Images

Disney Princess Hairstyles

- 40 Amazing Princess Hairstyles With Step by Step Images

Illustrations pages 6-11 © Aadarsh Pvt limited

Author: Theodora Mjoll Skuladottir Jack

Photographer: Gassi.is

Set designer and stylist: Ellen Lofts

Layout and design: Bjarney Hinriksdottir

Cover design: Gassi.is

Editors: Tinna Proppe, tinna@eddausa.com and Greta Bjorg Jakobsdottir

Printed in Slovenia

Distributed by Midpoint Book Sales & Distribution

Second Edition

ISBN 978-1-94078-703-9

www.eddausa.com

Hello dear reader

Welcome to the wonderful and magical
world of the Disney Princesses. Join us in creating
the amazing hairstyles of Ariel, Belle, Aurora, Rapunzel,
Mulan, Pocahontas, Merida, Tiana, Cinderella, Snow White
and Jasmine. In this book you will find hairstyles for all the
princesses with step by step photographs and instructions.
We encourage you to try as many hairstyles as you can and
use them as inspiration to create your own look, you can
even mix some of the styles together to create a new one.
We hope you enjoy taking this adventure with us!

Have fun!

List of contents:

Braidschool

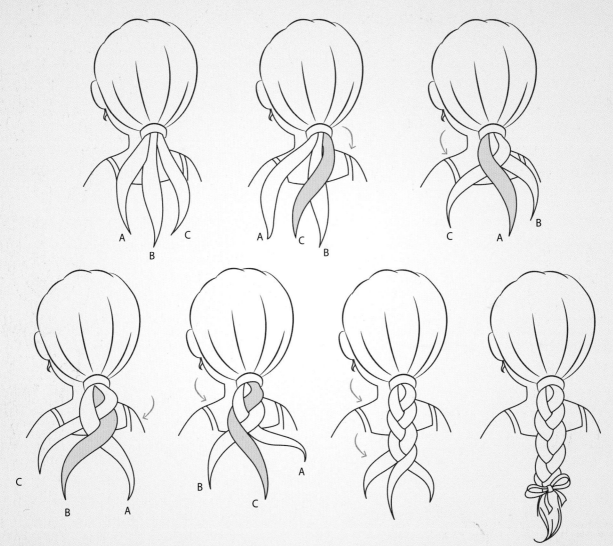

Traditional Braid

1. Divide the ponytail into three parts.
2. Move the lock of hair on the right over the lock in the middle.
3. Now take the lock of hair on the left and move it over the one that is in the middle.
4. Move the lock of hair that's now on the right, over the one in the middle.
5. Repeat this process until the whole ponytail has been braided.

French Braid

1. Take three locks of hair along the hairline in the front.
2. Move the lock of hair on the right over the lock in the middle.
3. Now take the lock of hair on the left and move it over the one that is in the middle.
4. Take the lock of hair on the right and add a small lock of hair from the head next to it, to the lock.
5. Move the lock of hair on the right along with the added hair over the lock of hair in the middle.
6. Repeat this process to the lock of hair on the left.
7. Repeat this process all the way down or until all the hair on the head has been added to the braid.
8. When all the hair has been added to the braid, make a traditional braid down the length of the hair.

Dutch Braid

1. Take three locks of hair along the hairline in the front.
2. Move the lock of hair on the right under the lock in the middle.
3. Now take the lock of hair on the left and move it under the one that is in the middle.
4. Take the lock of hair on the right and add a small lock of hair from the head next to it, to the lock.
5. Move the lock of hair on the right along with the added hair under the lock of hair in the middle.
6. Repeat this process to the lock of hair on the left.
7. Repeat this process all the way down or until all the hair on the head has been added to the braid.
8. When all the hair has been added to the braid, make a traditional braid down the length of the hair.

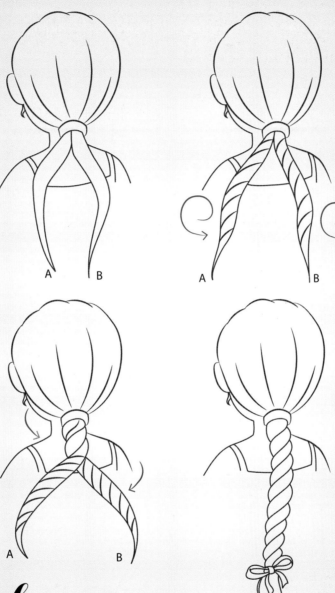

Rope Braid

1. Divide the ponytail in two.
2. Twist both locks in the same direction.
3. When both locks have been twisted a little bit cross them once in the opposite direction to the twist.
4. Keep twisting the locks in the same direction as before and cross the locks in the opposite direction to the twist.
5. Repeat the process down the length of the hair.

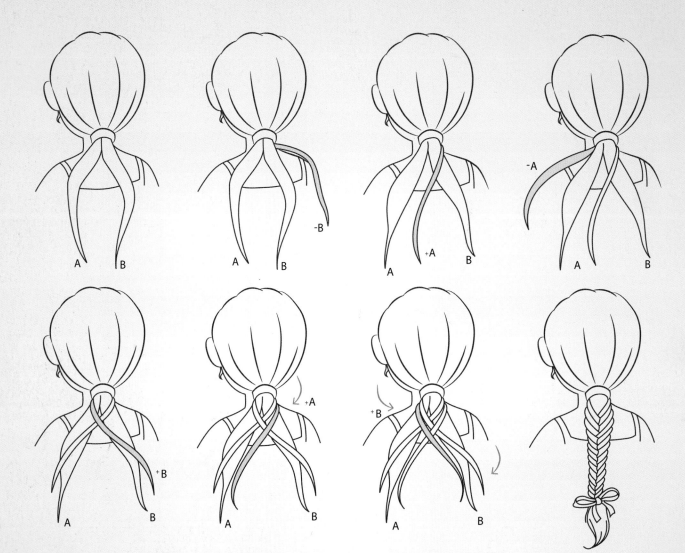

Traditional Fishtail Braid

1. Take two locks of hair along the hairline in the front.
2. Take a small lock of hair from the head just beside the big lock on the right and move it over the big lock and combine it with the big lock of hair to the left.
3. Now take a small lock of hair from the head just beside the big lock of hair on the left and move it over to the lock of hair on the right.
4. Take another small lock of hair from the head beside the big lock on the right and move it over the lock of hair on the left.
5. Repeat this process down the head until all the hair has been added to the braid.
6. When all the hair has been added to the braid, continue on by braiding a traditional fishtail braid down the length of the hair.

French Fishtail Braid

1. Take two locks of hair along the hairline in the front.
2. Take a small lock of hair from the head just beside the big lock on the right and move it over the big lock and combine it with the big lock of hair to the left.
3. Now take a small lock of hair from the head just beside the big lock of hair on the left and move it over to the lock of hair on the right.
4. Take another small lock of hair from the head beside the big lock on the right and move it over the lock of hair on the left.
5. Repeat this process down the head until all the hair has been added to the braid.
6. When all the hair has been added to the braid, continue on by braiding a traditional fishtail braid down the length of the hair.

Ariel

Hairstyles:

Locks of the Ocean

1. Take hold of a fairly large lock of hair at the front on one side.
2. Braid down the lock (see the Braidschool, p. 8).
3. Hold one part of the braid in one hand and the other two in the other hand.
4. Slide the two parts together up the lock.
5. Don't be afraid to slide it high up.
6. Pull the parts back down a little way and tie off the end with an elastic band.
7. Fix the locks of hair to even out the gaps between the twists.
8. Repeat the whole process on the other side of the head and join the finished locks in an elastic band at the back of the head.

Ariel's Braided Bun

1. Make a very deep side part at the front. Take aside the hair from the side part down to the ear on the other side. Gather the hair at the back in a ponytail.
2. Take three little locks of hair directly above the side part and start braiding a Dutch Braid (see the Braidschool, p. 10).
3. Braid as close to the forehead as possible.
4. Braid all the way down the hair and fasten the end with an elastic band.
5. To add volume, pull the sides of the braid apart.
6. Take the end of the braid and make a spiral close to the head.
7. Fix the spiral and hold it down with one hand when you are happy with its form.
8. Pin the braid spiral down. It works well to hook the braid and the hair below with the pin and then press it in. This way the hairstyle is secure without the pins showing.

Under the Sea

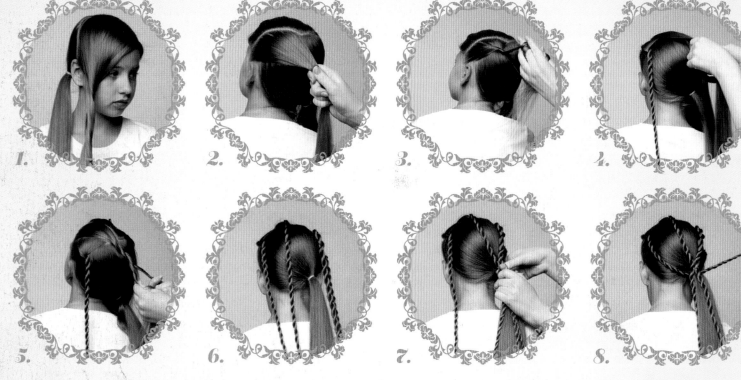

1. Divide the hair in two parts, horizontally across the back of the head. Gather the lower section in a low side ponytail.
2. Make a diagonal part for a quarter of the hair in the upper part, heading for the side ponytail.
3. Divide this part in two and make a rope braid (see the Braidschool, p. 11).
4. Fasten the end with an elastic band.
5. Part similarly next to the first part and repeat the process.
6. Repeat the whole process four times in the upper half.
7. Add three of the rope braids to the ponytail with a small elastic band, leaving the first rope out.
8. Place the loose rope braid under the ponytail and wrap it around the elastic.
9. Secure the rope braid with bobby pins.

Riding the Waves

1. Take hold of three locks of hair at the top of the head.
2. Start making a Dutch braid (see the Braidschool, p. 10).
3. When the first loop of the braid is ready, take a small section from it on the right side.
4. Continue braiding, but when reaching the same stage as before, take another small section from the braid on the right hand side.
5. Continue similarly down the braid, which should be made diagonally down the head.
6. Fasten the end of the braid with an elastic band.
7. Take hold of the two top sections from the braid.
8. Weave the sections tightly together close to the braid by crossing them repeatedly over one another.
9. Add sections to the twist on the way down the braid.
10. When you reach the end, fasten it with an elastic band.

Aurora

Hairstyles:

Aurora's Waves

1. Section the hair in two, horigontally across the top of the head. Make a side part in the hair in the front and clip the two parts away from the back section.
2. Start at the bottom of the lower section. Make a thin part. Put the curling tongs (medium sized) underneath the lock and wrap the hair around them.
3. Carefully, slide the tongs out of the lock.
4. Make another part above the first one and repeat the curling process. Do this all the way up this section.
5. Refrain from playing with the curled section until it has cooled down.
6. Now start on one side of the head. Make a horigontal part and curl in the same way as before.
7. Repeat this process, working up the head.
8. Finish up by the side part.
9. Now repeat the same process on the other side of the head.
10. Curl the hair all the way up to the side part.
11. When the hair has cooled down, comb it thoroughly again and again with a hairbrush, so that pretty waves form in the hair. Finish off with hairspray (take care not to apply too much).

Awakening the Forest

1. Make a side part in the front. Comb the hair on both sides of the face over it. Put a hairband over the hair in front of the ears.
2. Take the hair in front of the ears on one side and twist it.
3. When the lock of hair has been thoroughly twisted, hold one end with one hand and pull the twist with the other hand to increase its volume and shape.
4. It works well to let the child hold the twist while making a similar twist on the other side of the head.
5. Join the two twists at the back of the head.
6. Tie them with an elastic band.
7. Twist the hair from the small ponytail at the back below the secured twists and form a rose around the elastic band.
8. Pin the rose down by hooking a bobby pin into the rose and the hair underneath and press in.

Magical Locks

1. Divide the hair in two parts, horizontally, across the top of the head. Divide the upper part in two equal parts. A pintail comb works well to get a clean part.
2. Put a high ponytail in the section on the right.
3. Do the same on the left.
4. Lift one of the ponytails and stick the end of a topsy tail™ a little hairstyling tool seen in picture, under the elastic band.
5. Put the hair from the ponytail into the loop of the topsy tail™.
6. Pull the topsy tail™ with the hair up through the ponytail.
7. Allow the hair to fall down over the back.
8. Do the same on the other side.

Twist and Turn

1. Make an arch part for the fringe in the front. Pin the rest of the hair away.
2. Divide the section in two and backcomb lightly by the root.
3. Lay the hair diagonally down along the face and comb the surface of the hair well so that the backcombing becomes invisible.
4. Place the index finger and the middle finger under the lock.
5. Wrap the lock once around the fingers, up against the forehead.
6. Pin the bulge down with bobby pins, hooked into the bulge and the underlay of hair in the front.
7. Loosen the rest of the hair and combine with the hairstyle.

Belle

Hairstyles:

Belle's Bow

1. Take two locks of hair from both sides in the front and twist them.
2. Join the two locks in the back with a small elastic band.
3. Put another elastic band around the ponytail and form a loop by pulling half the lock down from the elastic band.
4. Divide the loop in two and bring the hair from the ponytail over the twist that you made first.
5. Bring the hair from the ponytail once around the middle of the loop that you made and back behind the twist.
6. Pin the ponytail completely down next to the knot that has formed.
7. Now fix the bow by pulling its loops to opposite sides.

Endless Braid

1. Take hold of three locks from the front by the face and start making a French braid (see the Braiding School, p. 9).
2. Continue the braid straight down the head and fasten it with an elastic band at the end.
3. To add volume, pull the sides of the braid apart.
4. Place the unattached braid against the attached one and fold in the end to hide it.
5. Pin the braid down with bobby pins, catching both the unattached braid and the French braid and press the pins in. Do this on both sides until the hairstyle is secure.

Ponytail with a Twist

1.   Loosely twist the hair on each side of the head and gather all the hair in a low ponytail.
2.   Form a hole above the elastic band.
3.   Slowly pull the ponytail through the hole.
4.   When all the hair is through, divide it in two and pull apart so that the elastic moves higher up.
     Pull the hair on the sides as you wish.

Cinderella

Hairstyles:

Cinderella's Bun

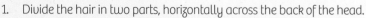

1. Divide the hair in two parts, horizontally across the back of the head.
2. Put the lower part in a high ponytail.
3. Place a hair doughnut around the ponytail and lightly pin it to the hair underneath. Divide the ponytail in two.
4. Wrap one part around the doughnut.
5. Pin it down. It works well to hook the hair and doughnut in the hair underneath to fasten the bun securely.
6. Now wrap the other part of the ponytail around the doughnut in the opposite direction from before.
7. Pin the hair down securely
8. Put a pretty hairband over the hair at the front.
9. Take the hair from one side and bring it to the back and up along the bun.
10. Fasten the ends of the hair up against the bun and take the hair from the other side.
11. Repeat the process from before.
12. Fix the hair, pin it down and spray at will.

Tie the Knot

1. Make a center part.
2. Make a horizontal part across the back of the head and put both the upper parts in high ponytails.
3. Wrap the ponytail on the right around the left one.
4. Now put it under the hair in the middle.
5. Wrap the end of the ponytail around the elastic band, and carefully pin it down.
6. Now take hold of the left ponytail.
7. Lift the right ponytail a little out of the way and pull the left ponytail through.
8. Wrap the left ponytail around the elastic of the right one.
9. Lift the whole middle of the hairstyle up and push the hair through.
10. Pin the end carefully down.

Buns and Braids

1. Divide the hair in two parts, horizontally across the back of the head. Pin the lower part away but leave the upper part loose.
2. Make a French braid (see the Braidschool, p. 9) down along the right side of the hair.
3. Braid all the way down the length and fasten with an elastic band at the end.
4. Repeat the process on the other side.
5. Gather the lower section in two low ponytails. It works well if the part is not too clean.
6. Place the index finger and the middle finger together under one of the ponytails and hold the ends with the other hand.
7. Twist the hair around with your fingers. Do not release the ends of the ponytail.
8. Once a pretty bun has been formed, release one hand and hold the bun in place with the other hand. Pin down the bun by hooking the pin in the edges of the bun and the bottom, and pressing it in.
9. Repeat the process with the other ponytail.
10. Bring the two braids back to the buns and pin them above. It works well to tuck the ends of the braids into the buns to hide them.

Jasmine

Hairstyles:

Jasmine's Ponytail

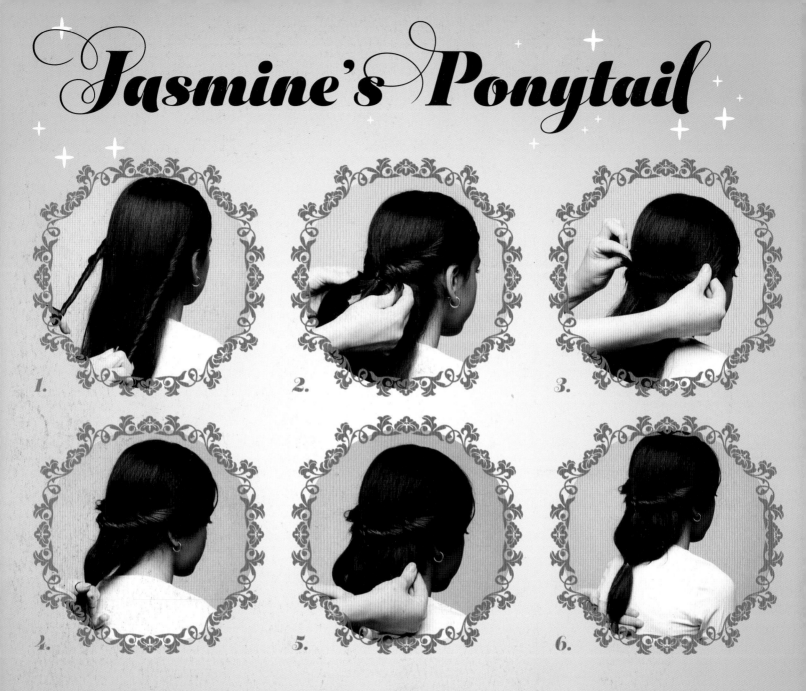

1. Take fairly large locks of hair from both sides of the head and twist them.
2. Join the twists at the back of the head and tie them with an elastic band.
3. Pull the twists out at will.
4. Tie the hair with an elastic band half-way down the length.
5. Pull the hair out at the sides.
6. Tie another elastic band at the bottom and pull the hair in between out at the sides.

Lower Bun

1. Put a pretty hairband over the head.
2. Stick two fingers under the hairband on the side and take hold of a lock in front.
   Slide the hair over and under the hairband.
3. Do the same on the other side.
4. Repeat the process along the hairband in the back for the whole length of the hair.
5. Fix and pull at will.

Twist from the East

1. Divide the hair into four equally large sections. Clip the two lower sections securely away from the face.
2. Take two little locks in one of the upper sections, close to the part at the back of the head. Criss-cross the two locks over one another.
3. Add hair to the first two locks with hair from their sides. Criss-cross the locks, and the extra hair, in the same way as before.
4. Continue with this method and move to the side of the child after a few repetitions. The twist moves along the back of the head, creating a wreath-like formation.
5. When the wreath has almost reached the ear, loosen the section directly below.
6. Take a lock from the lower section and move it into the twist. Continue in this fashion down the head.
7. Tie off the end with an elastic band close to the roots and repeat the process on the other side.
8. Join the two ponytails with one elastic band and fasten a pretty hair decoration into the joint.

High Ponytail

1. Gather all the hair in a high ponytail. Take a small lock of hair from the ponytail.
2. Wrap the small lock around the elastic band to conceal it.
3. Pin the end down by pressing the bobby pin in and under the elastic band.
4. Put a small elastic band around the ponytail a few centimeters down from it.
5. Put another similar elastic band around the ponytail at the same distance as before.
6. Repeat down the ponytail and pull the sides of the hair in between the elastic bands.
7. Be brave pulling the hair in between the elastic bands in all directions.

Merida

Hairstyles:

Topsy Turvy

1.

2.

3.

4.

5.

6.

7.

8.

9.

1. Make a center part from the forehead to the back of the head. A pintail comb works well for a clean parting.
2. Use the end of the comb to create a line from the end of the middle parting approximately to the cheekbone.
3. Put an elastic band around this section.
4. Repeat on the other side of the middle parting.
5. Stick the end of a topsy tail™ down into one ponytail, above the elastic band.
6. Put the hair from the ponytail through the topsy tail™.
7. Pull the topsy tail™ with the hair through.
8. Tighten the ponytail.
9. Do the same thing on the other side.

Curls for the Brave

1.

2.

3.

4.

5.

6.

1. Divide the hair horizontally across the nape of your neck. Pin the hair above and away.
2. Take a small lock of hair, place curling tongs under it and wrap the hair around the tongs. Start as close to the hair roots as you can.
3. Slide the curling tongs out of the lock.
4. Repeat throughout the section.
5. Divide the hair again horizontally, directly above the last parting and repeat the process with the tongs. Work your way up the head this way and finish with the hair at the front.
6. When all the hair has become curly, shake it out thoroughly with your fingertips.

Rough and Tough

1. 2.
3. 4.

1. Part all the hair in a rough zigzag.
2. Put a ponytail in both parts at the top of the head.
3. Roughly gather the hair from one of the ponytails and pin it down around it.
4. Repeat on the other side. It works well to combine the hair from the two ponytails.

Mulan

Hairstyles:

A Bun and a Half

1. Divide the hair in two across the top of the head and put the top half in a high ponytail.
2. Put a doughnut around the ponytail and fasten it with 2 or 3 bobbypins.
3. Put one hand firmly on top of the ponytail and wrap the hair around the doughnut with the other hand.
4. Be careful to hold the hair firmly while you wrap it around the doughnut so that it will look nice.
5. When all of the ponytail has been wrapped around the ponytail, fasten the end of the hair to the bun with a bobby pin.
6. If needed, fix the hair in the bun so it has the shape you wish.

Mulan's Bun

1. Gather all the hair in a high ponytail.
2. Tie a pretty ribbon around the elastic band with a knot.
3. Take one end of the ribbon with the hair, leaving the other end loose. Divide the hair in two and use the ribbon for the third part of the braid.
4. Braid the ribbon and the hair together down the length of the ponytail. Tie with an elastic band at the end.
5. Make a bun out of the braid up by the elastic band.
6. Take both ends of the ribbon and tie a knot.
7. Fix the ribbon as you please and cut it to size.

Battle of Twists and Turns

1. 2. 3. 4. 5. 6. 7. 8. 9. 10. 11.

1. Make a box like division in the hair on the top of the head and fasten the rest of the hair with a clip.
2. Take a lock of hair along the hairline and make a horizontal division and put the rest of the big lock in a clip.
3. Put a small elastic band in the small lock by the end of the box like division.
4. Take another lock just behind the first one and put an elastic band in it as before.

5. Repeat the process along the top of the hair until all the lock has been put into elastic bands.
6. Take a topsy tail™ and put it under the elastic band.
7. Put the hair from the small lock and put it into the hole in the topsy tail™.
8.-9. Pull the topsy tail™ all the way through the ponytail.
10. Make the ponytail a bit firmer.
11. Repeat the process along the top of the hair

Zik and Zak

1.–2. Divide all the hair in two along the middle of the hair.

3. Put one half of the hair in a clip and set it aside. Position the pintail comb on top of the head and draw a straight line down to the ear.

4. Put the lock in a ponytail.

5. Taka another lock below the previous one and make the division with the pintail comb.

6. Put the hair in a ponytail as before.

7. Now take the rest of the hair and put it in a low ponytail.

8. Repeat the process on the other half of the hair. After that you should have 6 ponytails around the head.

9. Twist the ponytail on the top of the head to the left and move it down to the ponytail in the middle on the right.

10. Combine the two ponytails by adding the middle ponytail into the twist and continue twisting.

11. Continue twisting the ponytail and move along to the low ponytail on the left and combine the twist with the last ponytail by putting them in an elastic band.

12. Repeat the process on the other side of the head.

Pocahontas

 Hairstyles:

Pocahontas's Hidden Braid

1. Divide the hair in two parts, horizontally across the back of the head. Gather the lower part in a ponytail.
2. Make a French braid (see the Braidschool, p. 9) with the upper part. Start at the front by the forehead.
3. Braid all the way down the length.
4. Fasten with an elastic band at the end.
5. Undo the ponytail in the lower section and divide in two.
6. Criss-cross the two parts over the braid, under it, and over again.
7. Join the braid and the two parts with an elastic band at the end.

Waterfall of Hair

1.   Take hold of three locks of hair on top of a side part at the front.
2.   Start making a French braid (see the Braidschool, p. 9). Each time the lock closest to the face goes into the braid, put half of it aside and leave it behind so that it falls down the side of the head.
3.   Take another lock from underneath the one that got left behind, and continue braiding.
4.   Repeat the process.
5.   Continue similarly down the side of the head.
6.   ...and along the back of the head.
7.   When you have gone all around, make a normal braid down the length.
8.   Put an elastic band at the end.

Rope of Hair

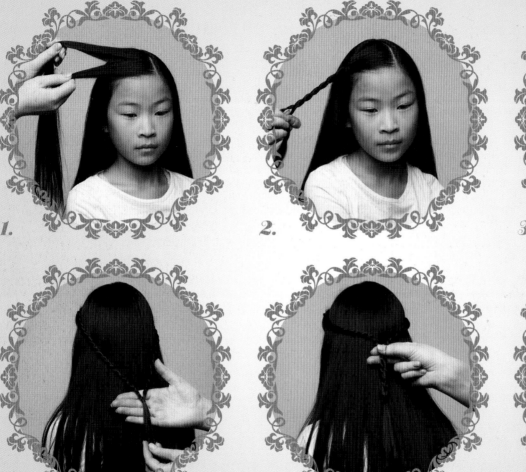

1. Take hold of a large lock of hair next to a side part at the front and divide it in two.
2. Make a rope braid from it (see the Braidschool, page 11).
3. Make the rope braid all the way down the length. Repeat the process on the other side of the head.
4. Join the two rope braids with an elastic band.
5.-6. Put another elastic band higher up in the ropes so that they join at the back of the head.

Fishbraid for Pocahontas

1. Make a side part. Take hold of the hair, all the way from the top of the part to the back of the head. The parting runs diagonally over the head. Pin the back part away.
2. Start a French fishtail braid (see the Braidschool, p 13) at the top by the side part.
3. Braid the fishtail all the way down along the hairline.
4. Braid a traditional fishtail down the length of the hair.
5. Loosen the hair at the back and bring the fishtail braid across it.
6. Fold in the end of the fishtail braid to hide it.
7. Fasten the braid to the side of the hair by hooking bobby pins in the braid and to the hair underneath and press the pins in against the braid.

Pocahontas's Braided Bun

1.   Begin by making a "horseshoe" part and put the hair on top in a side ponytail.
2.   Braid the ponytail and tie the end with an elastic band.
3.   Wrap the braid around the elastic band and flatten the bun. Pin it down securely.
4.   Tuck the end of the braid under the braided bun to hide it.

Rapunzel

Hairstyles:

Endless Curls

4.

5.

6.

1.

2.

3.

1. Start at the bottom and clip the rest of the hair.
2. Place the medium sized curling tongs facing diagonally down and wrap a medium sized lock around the tongs. Start by the roots of the hair and work down the length.
3. When the bottom section has all been curled, make another part above the first.
4. Curl in the same manner as before.
5. Continue with this method up along the head. Make a deep side part in the hair on top and curl the hair in the front away from the face to form a pretty sway.
6. Shake the hair thoroughly and use hairspray or other hair products if necessary.

Rapunzel's Full Braid

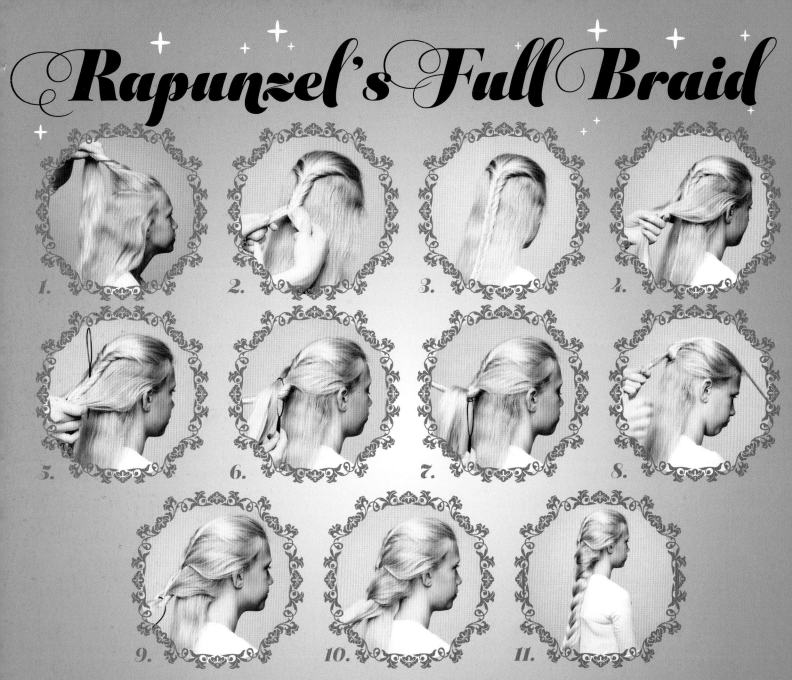

1. 2. 3. 4.
5. 6. 7. 8.
9. 10. 11.

1. Make a "horseshoe" part and take hold of the hair on top.
2. In that section make a fishtail braid all the way down the length (see the Braidschool, p. 12).
3. Tie the end with an elastic band.
4. Take hold of two large locks of hair from either side of the head.
5. Stick a topsy tail™ high in the fishtail.
6. Put the locks from the sides through the eye of the topsy tail™.
7. Pull the topsy tail™ with the locks through the fishtail.
8. Lift the fishtail away and join the locks with a small elastic band.
9. Take another two locks, in similar size to earlier locks, below the first locks. Stick the topsy tail™ into the fishtail. Pull it through with the locks as before. Try to keep the gap between the locks equal in length.
10. Continue with this method down the fishtail braid.
11. When you have reached all the way down, put an elastic band at the end.

Flower Girl

1.

2.

3.

4.

5.

6.

1. Divide the hair into three equally large sections.
2. Make a fishtail braid in the middle section all the way down (see the Braidschool, p. 12).
3. Make a fishtail braid in the other two sections just like the first one.
4. To add volume and an interesting shape, pull the sides of the braids apart.
5. Braid the three fishtails traditionally together (see the Braidschool, p. 8).
6. Tie the end with an elastic band and decorate with flowers.

Crown of Hair

1. Divide the hair close to the middle in the front. Take a large lock of hair from the back of the head towards the face.
2. Braid the lock along the face down the length of the hair and tie with an elastic band at the end.
3. Do the same on the other side.
4. Take one of the braids and bring it across the forehead to the back.
5. Pin the braid down in the back. For strong hold, press the bobby pin against the braid.
6. Take the other braid to the other side and back, in the same manner as before.
7. Fasten its end in the same way as before.

Snow White

Hairstyles:

Red Ribbon

1.

2.

3.

5.   6.   7.   8.

9.   10.

1. Take hold of a small lock of hair, close to the face in the middle. Fasten a long ribbon to the lock with an elastic band.
2. Now make a side part in the hair and put the hair over the ribbon. Take hold of a lock by the part with one hand and hold the ribbon with the other.
3. Wrap the lock once around the ribbon. The lock now appears closer to the face and the ribbon away from the face.
4. Add hair to the lock and wrap it once around the ribbon.
5. Repeat the process, taking care of how the hair falls into the twist.
6. Wrap the lock around the ribbon each time hair is added.
7. Continue this method down along the hairline.
8. When all the hair has been added to the twist, tie the hair and the ribbon with an elastic band close to the roots.
9. Fold the ribbon and tie it around the elastic band.
10. Tie the ribbon into a bow.

Snow White's Bun and Braid

1. Make a side parting in the front and draw a line from the parting in a curve along the top of the head.
2. Put the rest of the hair in a low ponytail.
3. Divide the lock of hair in the front in two.
4. Make a Dutch braid (see the Braidschool, p. 10) in the back half of the lock all the way down the length of the lock.
5. Pull the braid out the sides to increase it's volume.
6. Create a hole above the elastic band in the low ponytail.
7. Pull the ponytail through the hole.
8. Pull the whole ponytail again through the hole and divide the ends of the ponytail in two.
9. Fasten the two halves on each side of the bun that has formed, this will create a nice long bun. Use bobby pins to fasten.
10. Take the loose lock in the front and move it backwards towards the bun.
11. Fasten the lock with pins and hide the end of it inside the bun.
12. Do the same with the braid. Pull on the hair and the bun to get the desired look.

Braid of Braids

1. Make a deep side part in the hair.
2. Take three small locks above the side part and make a Dutch braid (see the Braidschool, p. 10) along the hairline.
3. Try to make the braid as close to the hairline as possible.
4. Continue along the rest of the hairline, or until all the hair has been gathered into the braid. Then make a traditional braid down the length.
5. Wrap the braid in a circle up against the side of the head, and pin the bun down by hooking bobby pins into the braid and the hair underneath and press it in.

Tiana

Hairstyles:

Tiana's Bun

1. Put all the hair up in a high ponytail.
2. Put a hair doughnut around the ponytail and pin it down loosely.
3. Distribute the hair from the ponytail evenly over the doughnut and pin the hair against the doughnut. It works well to fold the hair into the doughnut to conceal the ends.
4. Pin the hair securely all the way around.

Around the World

1. Make a circular part in the middle of the head and pin the hair down carefully.
2. Divide the upper section in two pieces.
3. Twist the hair in one of the sections close to the roots down along the head.
4. Continue down along the circle and bend the twist in a circle towards the other section.
5. When the twist has been bent into a circle, loosen the hair around the middle.
6. Bring the twist closer to the forehead by adding hair along the hairline at the front.
7. Continue the twist down alongside the forehead.
8. ...and all the way alongside the hairline at the back. Put a ponytail in the hair close to the roots.
9. Pull and form the hairstyle at will.

Braid Without Braiding

1. Gather the hair from closest to the forehead to the back of the head.
2. Pin the hair down by hooking a bobby pin into the locks and pushing it into the hair in the opposite direction. This way the pin is secured and cannot be seen.
3. Roughly gather the hair from the side that was left behind and criss-cross the locks one over the other below what you first did.
4. Carefully pin the hair using the same method as before.
5. Take another two similar locks from each side and move to the back of the head.
6. Pin the locks together, using the same method as before.
7. Repeat the process down the length, or until all the hair has been gathered in the hairstyle.
8. Tuck the ends in towards the nape of the neck if necessary and pin down.

 Index

Updos and Buns

 Waves and Ponytails

Twists and Braids

The
End